THE INDECENT REPRESENTATION OF WOMEN (PROHIBITION) ACT 1986

VOLUME 2, ISSUE 2 OF BRILLOPEDIA

P.ISHWARYA

DEDICATED TO MY MOTHER

Contents

Preface

"Start writing, no matter what. The water does not flow until the faucet is turned on".

-Louis L'Amour

Hundreds of students and professors are contributing their work to Brain Booster Articles, we are here to provide ample information about Law and Contemporary issues. Our aim is to provide a platform for today's generation to express their views and ideas on law and contemporary law.

Author

CHAPTER ONE

Abstract

During the Vedic era women were well treated by the people after some decades it was completely changed. There were a lot of crimes against women was emerged in society. On another side media indecently portrays women through advertisements, drawings, and photographs in front of people. To prohibit this kind of violation against women, the government enacted the legislation called the indecent representation of women (Prohibition) Act 1986. The object of the act is to punish the publishers and advertisers who indecently represent women through advertisements, pamphlets, books etc. Section 6 of the act talks about punishment for an offence mentioned under the act. In 1987 central government established certain rules to exercise power given under section 10 of the 1986 Act. The right to life under Article 21 of the Indian constitution is not merely a physical right but also a right to live with human dignity. After some years it will also become outdated due to social changes that occurred in society so, in 2012 indecent representation of women prohibition bill was introduced in front of parliament based on the recommendations given by the National Commission for women and observations made by the parliamentary standing committee. After the introduction of the 2012 bill, some clause of the 1986 Act was amended.

Introduction

The indecent representation of women (Prohibition) Act was enacted in 1986. The main object of the act is to punish publishers and advertisers who knowingly disseminate materials indecently portraying women.

Features of the Act:

1. This act applies to the whole of India.

2. It contains 10 sections.

2. To prohibit advertisements containing indecent representation of women.

3. Section – 4 deals with the prohibition of publication or sending by post of books, pamphlets, etc containing indecent representation of women.

4. Section- 6 of the act talks about punishment for offenders.

<u>Definitions</u>: section 2 of the Act deals with definitions for the certain term mentioned under the act

Section 2(a): advertisement

The definition of advertisement given under this act is not exhaustive. Advertisement includes notice, label, wrapper, or other documents and any visible representation through light, sound, smoke, or gas.

Section 2 (b): distribution

It is an inclusive definition. Distribution includes the distribution by the way of samples whether free or paid.

Section 2(c): indecent representation of women means the depiction regards the figure of women or form or body or any part which has the effect of being indecent, derogatory, denigrating them or is to deprave, corrupt, injure the public morality.

Section 2 (d): label

A label is defined as any written, marked, stamped, printed matter affixed to, or appearing upon a package.

Section 2 (e): package

It includes box, carton and tin.

Section 2 (f): prescribed

Prescribed defined as rules given under this act.

Section 3: prohibition of advertisements

Section 3 of the Act prohibits the publication or exhibition of advertisement which contains indecent representation of women.

Section 4:

Section 4 forbids any person to sell or let to hire, or distribute any indecent representation regards women in the form of books, pamphlets, drawings, photographs, and paintings.

Exception:

1)Any ancient monument is covered under the meaning of

the Ancient Monument and Archaeological Sites and Remains Act 1958.

2) Representation is in the interest of science, literature, art, or learning or which is kept or used for bona fide religious purposes.

3) Representation covers under Part – II of the cinematography Act 1952.

Section 5:Deals with the powers and rights of an authorized officer

If an authorized officer has reason to believe that an offence under this act is committed, he is entitled to enter and search in such places at any time.

He has the right to seize such indecent representation in the form of advertisements, paintings, drawings, photography, slide, figure, writing, or pamphlet.

He has the right to examine materials, records, and documents which furnish information regards the offence.

The authorized officer cannot enter a dwelling house without a warrant.

The criminal procedure code of 1973 has to refer to the seizure or a search of anything mentioned under the act.

If an authorized officer seized anything he has to inform such seizure to the nearby magistrate to receive an order of custody.

Section 6: penalty

Talks about punishment for an offence mentioned under this act.

If a person is convicted for the first time he may punish with imprisonment up to two years and with a fine which may extend to two thousand rupees incase of a second conviction he may punish with imprisonment for a term not less than six months which may extend to five years and with a fine which extends up to one lakh rupees.

Section 7

Talks about offences by the companies.if the indecent representation was committed by the company every person who was in charge of the company at that time will also be liable for an offence.

Exception:

1. An act is done without his knowledge.

2. If he had taken all due diligence to prevent the commission of an act.

The burden of proof lies on the offender.

Explanation:

Company

The term Company is defined as anybody corporate, a firm, or other association of individuals.

Director

Director means concerning a firm and a partner in the firm.

Section 8: The offence mentioned under this act is bailable and cognizable (code of criminal procedure, 1973 (2 of 1974).

Section 9: of the act protects action taken in good faith.

Section 10: of the act talks power to make rules by the central government through a notification in the official gazette.

Amendment:

The indecent representation of women amendment bill was introduced in 2012 based on the recommendations given by National Commission for women and observations made by the parliamentary standing committee.

A new Definition clause was included under the bill.

Section 2 (da):

Materials include any book, pamphlet, paper slide, painting, photograph, or content in printed, audio, visual, or electronic.

Section 2 (aa): electronic form.

Section 2 of the information technology act 2000 defined the term electronic form. The same meaning will also apply to the act.

Section 6 of the bill deals with punishment

The imprisonment term for the first conviction was increased from two years to three years and a fine may extend to one lakh rupees. and for subsequent conviction, the term imprisonment may extend up to seven years and the fine amount may extend up to five lakh rupees.

CHAPTER THREE

Case study

1. <u>Rajnitudeshivs the state of Maharashtra</u>

<u>Fact of the case</u>

Rajnitudhesi and his three partners were prosecuted for selling obscene books and copies of lady Chatterley's under section – 292 of the Indian penal code 1860.

<u>Issue of the case</u>

1. whether section – 292 of Indian penal code1860 violated Article 19 (1) (a) of the Indian constitution.
2. whether it comes under the purview of section 292 of Indian penal code1860.

<u>Argument by the respondent</u>

The accused contended that lady Chatterley's book does not have obscene content if we read it wholly.

<u>Judgement</u>

The supreme court held that the rajnitudeshi and other his three partners were liable for the selling of obscene books under section 292 of Indian penal code1860.

2. <u>Maneka Gandhi vs Union of India</u>

The supreme court held right to life under Article 21 of the Indian constitution is not merely a physical right but also a right to live with human dignity.

3. <u>Francis Coralie vs union territory of Delhi:</u>

In this case, the Supreme Court held that the right to life includes the right to live with human dignity. The indecent representation of women (Prohibition) Rules, 1987. In 1987 central government established certain rules to exercise powers conferred under section – 10 of the Act 1986. It contains five sections and came into force on 2nd October 1986.

Features of the Act:

1. Definition for the words article and authorised officer was given.
2. It established a manner of seizing articles.
3. section 4 of the Act talks about the manner of packing and dealing with seized things.

1. section 1 of the Act deals with short title and commencement.

2. Section 2 Talks about Definitions:

a) Act:

The term Act refers to The Indecent Representation of Women (Prohibition) Act,1986.

b) Articles:

The term articles are defined as books, pamphlets, paper, slide, film, writing, drawing, photograph, or representation of figure.

c) Authorized Officer:

The authorized officer is defined as any Gazetted officer authorised by the state.

d) Section:

Means section mentioned under the Act.

3. Section 3:

This section talks manner of seizing articles. The authorized officer after seizing advertisements or articles.

He should prepare a list of details containing a description, quality, quantity, and mark of seizure advertisements or articles.

A seized article or advertisement should be packed and sealed by the authorised officer and a copy of the list containing details of such seizure should be delivered to the person from whom they seized.

The seized articles or advertisements shall be marked with a distinguishing number and shall also be signed by the authorised officer. if it is not possible to mark the number on such advertisement or articles the authorised officer may follow any other manner.

4. section 4:

Sec 4 talks about the packing manner of seized articles or advertisements.

The seized advertisements or articles should be packed with either strong paper or cloth. While packing such seized articles or advertisement ends of the paper should not be tampered with.

After packing such articles or advertisements it should be affixed by either gum or stitched in or tied.

Further, the package should be sealed with wax and receive the impression from the authorized officer.

If necessary such advertisements or articles shall be put into a box or container by the authorised officer.

5. section 5: If the rules prescribed under the act are not possible to follow due to the nature of such advertisements or articles the authorized officer may follow any other manner without affecting its value.

CHAPTER FOUR

Conclusion

Even though having much legislation for the protection of women, still there is a lot of crimes against women occurring in our society. Good law can also become a bad law and a bad law can also become a good law it depends upon the executor of the law.

Suggestions

a) legislation should be updated as per the needs of the society.

b) imprisonment term and the fine amount should be increased.

c) speedy justice.